OUR FAVORITE VIDEO GAMES

THE SIMS

BY BETSY RATHBURN

EPIC

BELLWETHER MEDIA ◆ MINNEAPOLIS, MN

EPIC

EPIC BOOKS are no ordinary books. They burst with intense action, high-speed heroics, and shadows of the unknown. Are you ready for an Epic adventure?

This is not an official Sims book. It is not approved by or connected with Electronic Arts.

This edition first published in 2026 by Bellwether Media, Inc.

No part of this publication may be reproduced in whole or in part without written permission of the publisher. For information regarding permission, write to Bellwether Media, Inc., Attention: Permissions Department, 3500 American Blvd W, Suite 150, Bloomington, MN 55431.

Library of Congress Cataloging-in-Publication Data

LC record for The Sims available at: https://lccn.loc.gov/2025003630

Text copyright © 2026 by Bellwether Media, Inc. EPIC and associated logos are trademarks and/or registered trademarks of Bellwether Media, Inc. Bellwether Media is a division of FlutterBee Education Group.

Editor: Christina Leaf   Designer: Gabriel Hilger

Printed in the United States of America, North Mankato, MN.

TABLE OF CONTENTS

A SIM'S DAY 4

THE HISTORY OF THE SIMS 8

THE SIMS TODAY 18

THE SIMS FANS 20

GLOSSARY 22

TO LEARN MORE 23

INDEX 24

A SIM'S DAY

A Sim heads to work in a good mood. Their **charisma** just reached a new level. A notice pops up. The Sim is now a secret agent! Soon they can buy a **mansion**!

The Sims is a **series** of **simulation games**. It is made by a **developer** called Maxis.

Simlish

Sims speak their own language. It is called Simlish.

BUILDING A HOUSE

Players control the lives of characters called Sims. They build and **decorate** houses. They find jobs and friends!

THE HISTORY OF THE SIMS

The Sims was created by Will Wright. In the 1990s, a fire forced him to rebuild his home.

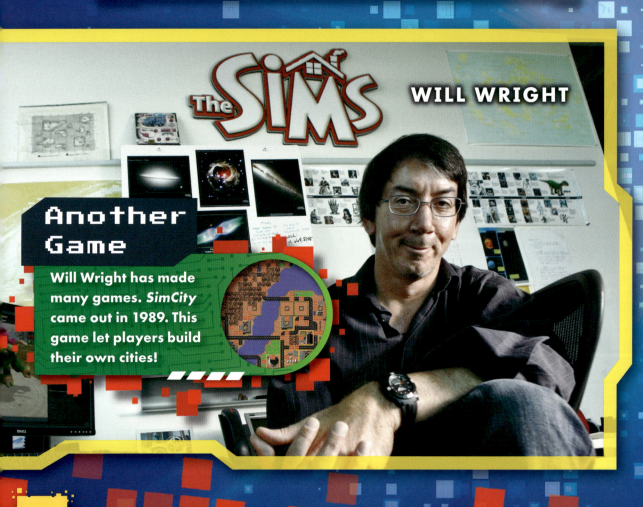

WILL WRIGHT

Another Game

Will Wright has made many games. *SimCity* came out in 1989. This game let players build their own cities!

This **inspired** a new game. *The Sims* came out in 2000.

DEVELOPER PROFILE

NAME: Maxis

LOCATION: Redwood City, California

YEAR FOUNDED: 1987

NUMBER OF EMPLOYEES: up to 500

Expansion packs were soon released. These added new items and ways to play. *The Sims: Unleashed* let Sims have pets! *The Sims Online* came out in 2002. It let people play online with others.

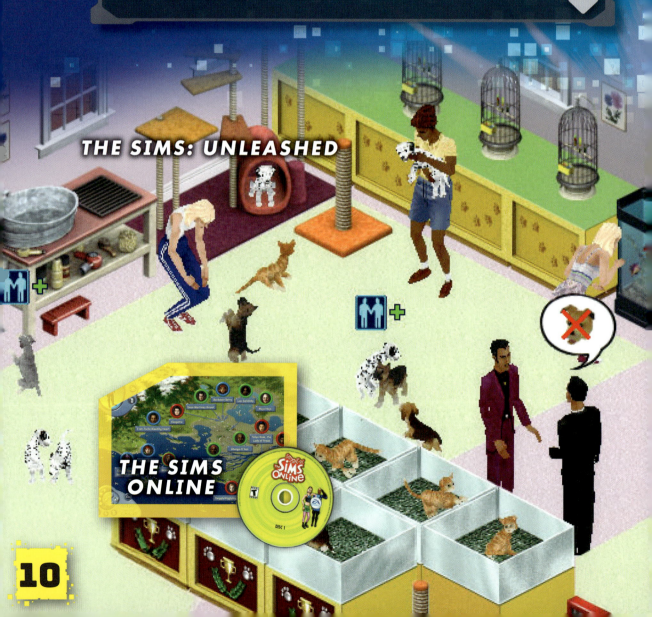

THE SIMS: UNLEASHED

THE SIMS ONLINE

EXPANSION PACKS

The Sims: Superstar

Released	2003
Addition	Sims can become famous

The Sims 2: Seasons

Released	2007
Additions	seasons, gardening

The Sims 3: World Adventures

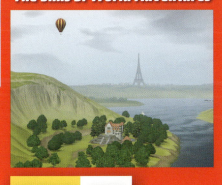

Released	2009
Addition	Sims can travel to different countries

The Sims 4: City Living

Released	2016
Additions	apartments, new festivals

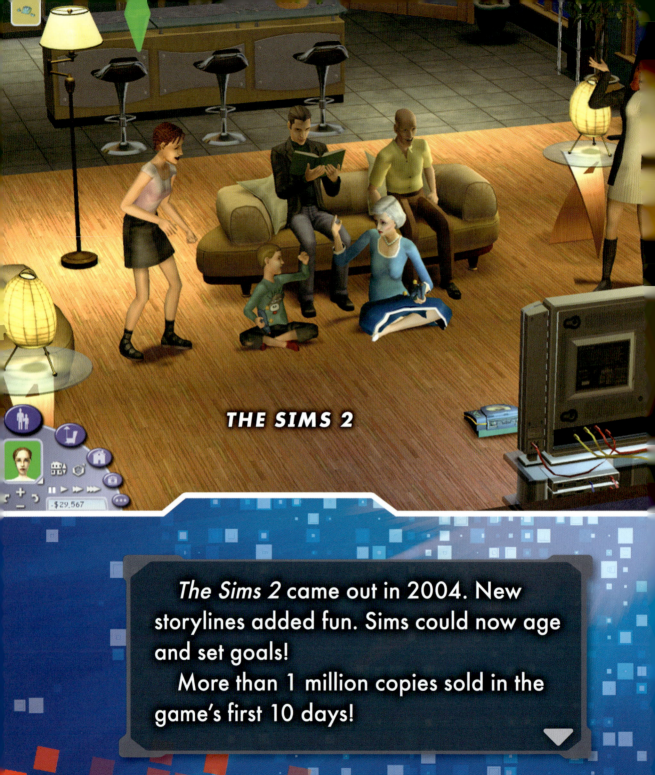

THE SIMS 2

The Sims 2 came out in 2004. New storylines added fun. Sims could now age and set goals!

More than 1 million copies sold in the game's first 10 days!

THE SIMS TIMELINE

2000
The Sims is released

2004
The Sims 2 is released

2009
The Sims 3 is released

2014
The Sims 4 is released

2022
Maxis makes The Sims 4 available for free

The Sims 3 was released in 2009. Players could **customize** their Sims more than ever. They could perfect looks and choose personalities.

THE SIMS 3

The game had an **open world**. Sims could explore their surroundings.

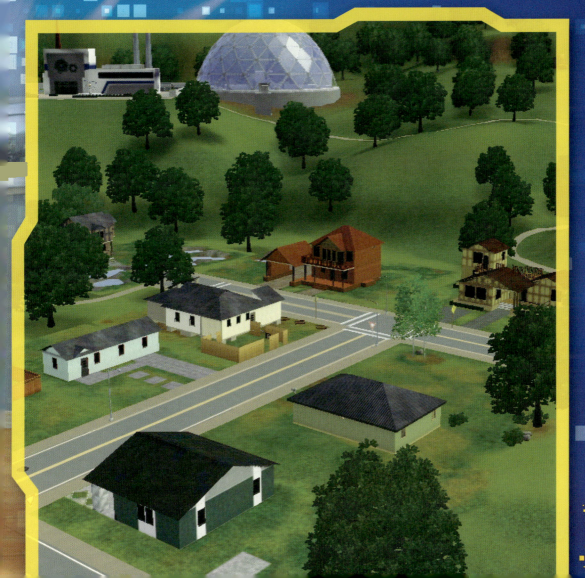

Stuff Packs

A "stuff pack" is a set of new items for Sims games. There are 20 stuff packs for *The Sims 4*. One adds new pets. Another adds haunted houses!

In 2014, *The Sims 4* was released. It made a Sim's emotions more important. A Sim's mood could affect their actions.

The Sims 4 became free to play in 2022. Players can buy extra expansions!

17

THE SIMS TODAY

Today, people can play Sims games on computers and **mobile devices**. They can also play on Xbox and PlayStation **consoles**.

HOURS OF *THE SIMS 4* PLAYED

18

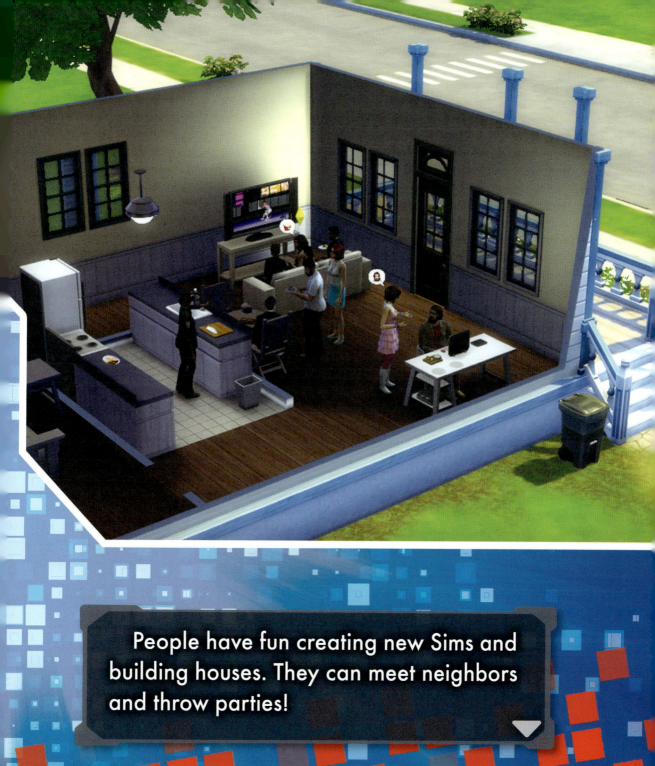

People have fun creating new Sims and building houses. They can meet neighbors and throw parties!

THE SIMS FANS

Sims fans can share their favorite Sims and homes online in the Gallery.

Some players use **mods**. Mods can add new storylines. They can add new items. There are many ways to have fun in Sims games!

POPULAR *THE SIMS 4* MOD

NAME	Ultimate Dancer Career
RELEASED	2018
DOWNLOADS	more than 300,000
WHAT IT DOES	players can have their Sims follow a dancer career track

GLOSSARY

charisma—a quality that makes someone seem more appealing to others

consoles—game systems that connect to TVs to play video games

customize—to make based on personal preferences

decorate—to make something look nice by adding beautiful things

developer—a company that makes video games

expansion packs—additions to video games that add extra content to the original game

inspired—gave someone an idea about what to do or create

mansion—a large house

mobile devices—devices such as smartphones that can be used almost anywhere

mods—changes users make to the original game

open world—a virtual world that players can move through freely

series—a number of related games

simulation games—games made to be like real life

TO LEARN MORE

AT THE LIBRARY

Galanin, Dennis. *The Amazing World of Video Game Development*. Sanger, Calif.: Familius, 2022.

Neuenfeldt, Elizabeth. *Video Games*. Minneapolis, Minn.: Bellwether Media, 2023.

Rathburn, Betsy. *Animal Crossing*. Minneapolis, Minn.: Bellwether Media, 2026.

ON THE WEB

FACTSURFER

Factsurfer.com gives you a safe, fun way to find more information.

1. Go to www.factsurfer.com.

2. Enter "The Sims" into the search box and click 🔍.

3. Select your book cover to see a list of related content.

INDEX

computers, 18
consoles, 18
expansion packs, 10, 11, 17
fans, 20
gallery, 20, 21
history, 8, 9, 10, 11, 12, 13, 14, 15, 16, 17
hours played, 18
houses, 4, 7, 19, 20
items, 10, 16, 20
Maxis, 6, 9
mobile devices, 18
mods, 20
players, 7, 10, 14, 17, 18, 19
sales, 12

Sim, 4, 5, 6, 7, 10, 12, 14, 15, 16, 19, 20
SimCity, 8
Simlish, 6
Sims, The, 9
Sims 2, The, 12
Sims 3, The, 14, 15
Sims 4, The, 16, 17, 18, 20
Sims Online, The, 10
simulation games, 6
stuff packs, 16
timeline, 13
Wright, Will, 8

The images in this book are reproduced through the courtesy of: SimsVIP/ Flickr, front cover; Sierra Thompson, pp. 3, 6 (all), 11 (*City Living*), 16-17, 21; Gabriel Hilger, pp. 7, 14, 15, 16 (all), 17 (inset), 19, 21 (Gallery); DC Studio/ AdobeStock, p. 4; Christina Leaf, pp. 5, 13 (2022); AFP/ Stringer/ Getty Images, p. 8 (Will Wright); Bayo/ Wikipedia, p. 8 (*SimCity*); Feng Yu, p. 9 (computer); Pete Jenkins/ Alamy Stock Photo, pp. 9 (*The Sims* cover), 13 (2000, 2004); Bloomberg/ Contributor/ Getty Images, p. 9 (Maxis); Beyond Sims/ Flickr, pp. 10 (all), 11 (*Superstar, Seasons, World Adventures*), 12; DatBot/ Wikipedia, p. 13 (2009); urbanbuzz, p. 13 (2014); asiashamecca, p. 20.